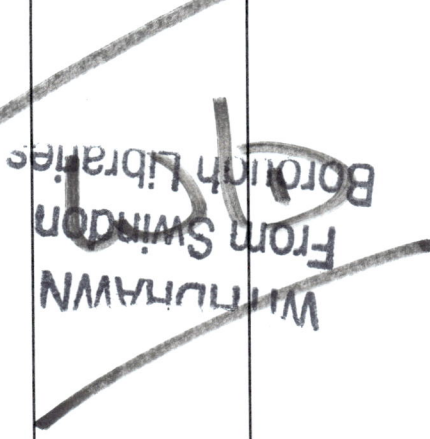

CONTENTS

GETTING STARTED

Even before spoken language, art was used to record ideas and facts; for example, scenes from Stone Age hunts were drawn on cave walls. Today, we draw for all sorts of reasons: to express our feelings and dreams, to tell stories, and even to help us navigate. (Where would we be without maps?)

This book contains 11 drawing projects for you to try, and each one includes advice and suggestions. There are tips to help you with techniques, but don't worry about making your drawing perfect – the most important thing is to let your imagination flow. Feel free to experiment and just have fun with the creative process. There are no rules, just suggestions. Build your skills through each project – you can start anywhere, skip pages and have a go at whatever inspires you!

PAPER, PENS AND PENCILS

Take a trip to an art suppliers and choose some of these materials to get you started. Each of these drawing tools produce different effects and can be used separately or together – the possibilities are fun and endless!

PAPER

Paper comes in different thicknesses, or weights, and textures. Unfinished paper is great for pencils and charcoal, while smooth Bristol paper is more suitable for pens and felt tips. For sketching, use a thicker paper that can cope with lots of rubbing out.

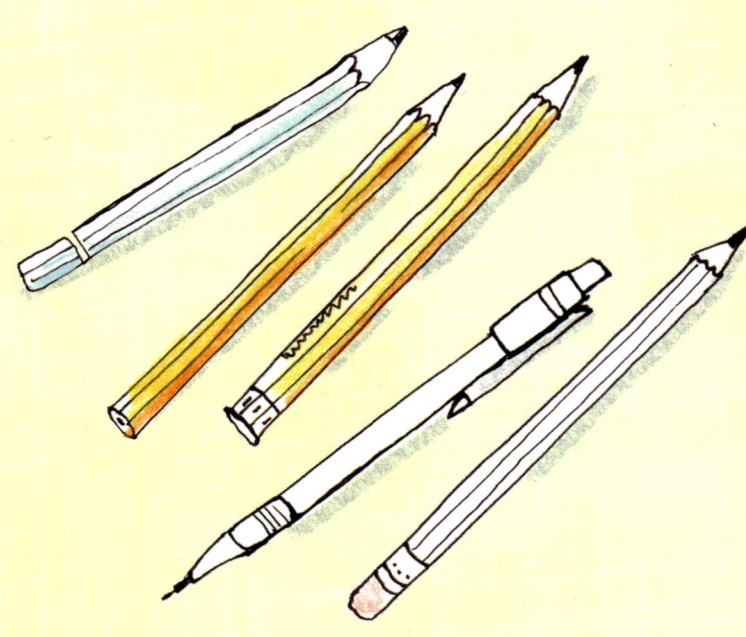

GRAPHITE PENCILS

These come in H and B categories. B pencils are soft; 4B is medium-soft and produces a good smudgy line, while 9B is very soft and better for covering bigger areas. H pencils are perfect for making finer, more detailed lines.

CHARCOAL PENCILS

These fragile black pencils are good for smudging, layering and blending – but they can get messy!

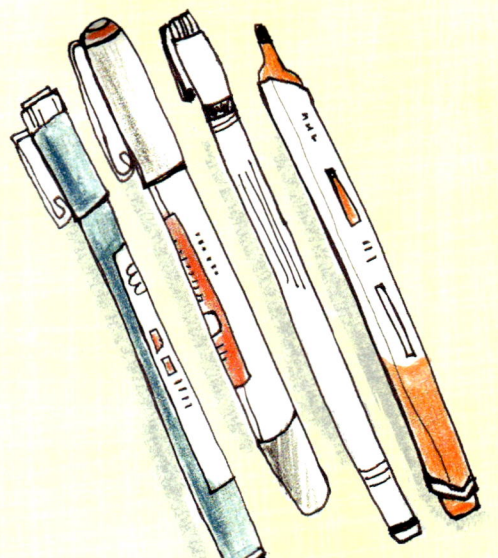

PENS

There are a huge variety of pens available, including biros, ballpoints, felt tips and brush pens, to name but a few. They are good for clear, neat lines, and come in permanent and water-based varieties. Try experimenting with different tips and brushes, from super-thick to super-thin, to see what effects you can achieve.

PASTELS AND CONTE CRAYONS

Try these for tools that are soft and versatile, and can produce clear lines as well as soft shading.

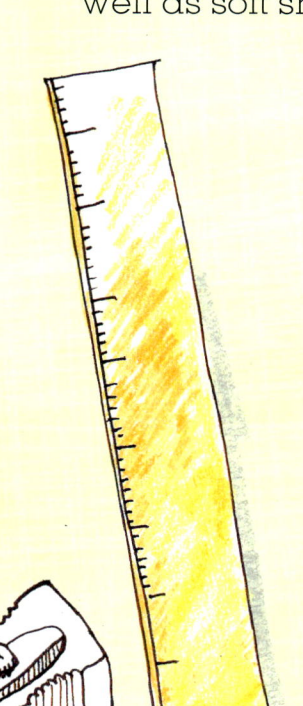

COLOURED PENCILS

These are waxier than graphite, and come in an amazing array of vibrant colours.

BITS AND BOBS

A pencil sharpener, rubber and ruler will also be very useful.

TOP TIPS

Before you get stuck into the drawing projects, here are some great tips that will help you throughout the book and beyond.

LOOK!
Observation is the most important part of learning to draw. Draw what you see rather than what you know. In order to do this, you need to look at what you're drawing a lot!

THINK NEGATIVE
Remember, negative space – the white space around objects – is just as important as positive space, or what we draw.

DON'T GIVE UP
There is no right and wrong, and some of the best artworks have come from happy accidents.

BE PREPARED FOR A CHALLENGE
Sometimes you will be disappointed, but painting over things can create new ideas.

GET TO KNOW YOUR EQUIPMENT
Experiment with different mark-making techniques and textures for each drawing tool.

PRACTISE, PRACTISE, PRACTISE!
Draw every day, and copy anything that catches your eye. Notice shapes, pattern, detail, features and colour.

THE COLOUR WHEEL

The colour wheel is really helpful for showing the relationship between different colours. Pick out different combinations from the wheel to create colour schemes for your drawings.

WARM COLOURS

COOL COLOURS

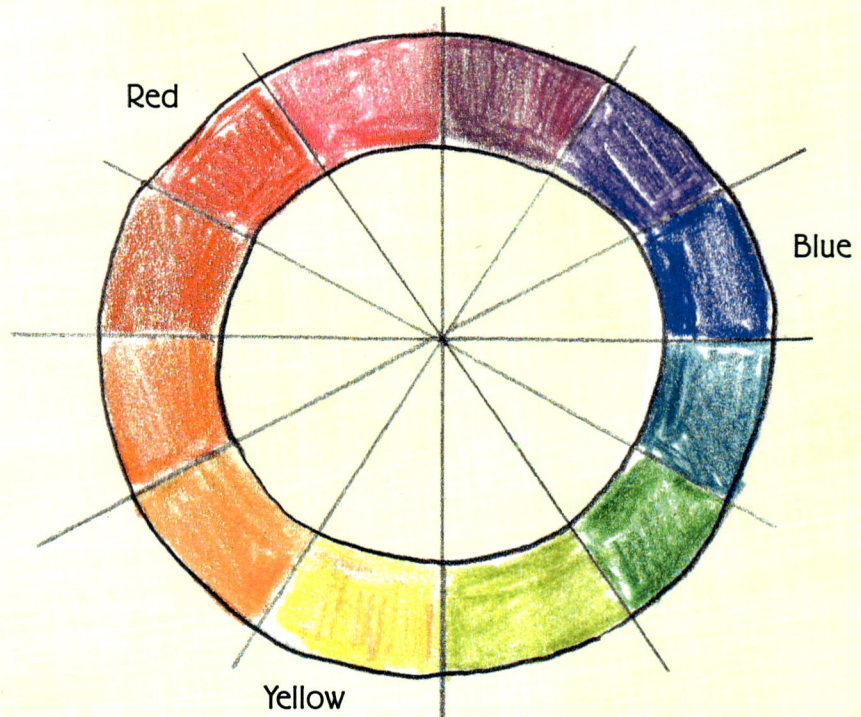

The primary colours are red, yellow and blue. The secondary colours are purple (blue and red), orange (red and yellow) and green (blue and yellow).

Colours next to each other on the colour wheel work in harmony with each other. They are called 'analogous colours'.

Colours opposite each other on the colour wheel are contrasting. They intensify each other and are called 'complementary colours'.

Warm colours, like red, orange and yellow, are vivid and energetic. Cool colours, like blue, green and purple, are calm and soothing.

GET DOODLING

Doodling is when you scribble playfully with no particular result in mind – it just comes from your imagination. Whatever pops into your head, just let one image lead into another.

When you doodle, there's no pressure to create a masterpiece; just let your mind (and your pencil) wander. No one will ever know if it doesn't come out like you planned! You can doodle anywhere, any time. You will soon become a demon doodler!

NOW TRY ...
CRAZY CREATURES

Start with the outlines of familiar animals, then let your imagination fly! What colour fur do the animals have? How many heads? Imagine how they might move – do they run, fly or even dig?

NOW TRY ... FLOWER POWER

Draw basic flower shapes as bold and rounded outlines, then fill them in with patterns. Try decorating each petal and leaf shape in a different way. Experiment with swirls, spirals, arrows, squiggles, clouds and whatever else you can dream up!

DRAWING ANIMALS

Drawing animals is great fun, but it can be daunting if you don't know where to start. Breaking them down into simple lines and shapes will be a big help.

Pick up a pencil and see if you can draw a dog by following these steps.

STEP 1
Start with a circular shape for the head and two black dots for eyes.

STEP 2
Now add more detail: a black nose and big floppy ears.

NOW TRY ...
THE THREE Fs

Different drawing tools are brilliant at creating all sorts of animal effects, such as fur, feathers and features.

FUR
Draw the textured fur of a lion using pastels and chunky strokes. Layer coloured pencil over the top to add detail.

STEP 3
Add the front legs ...

STEP 5
Then add the back legs.

Once you're confident creating the outline, start to experiment. Try drawing all sorts of dogs: big ones, small ones and spotty ones.

STEP 4
And now the body.

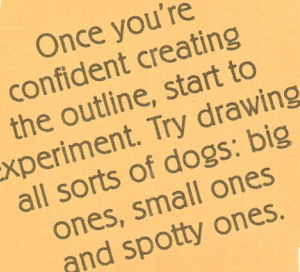

STEP 6
Put the tail on and you're finished!

FEATHERS
The super-vibrant colours from felt pens will bring a fabulous peacock tail to life. Brush pens have bendy tips, so you can get different line thicknesses for the bold feathers.

FEATURES
Draw an outline of a crazy croc using your favourite green pencil. Add scary teeth and other features with black pen.

CAPTURING FACES

Faces are the most expressive parts of people's bodies. When you get them right, you show a person's personality and emotions. They can be tricky to draw, but just like drawing animals, you can break a face down to make it less difficult.

STEP 1
Sketch an oval with one line across and one line down the middle.

STEP 2
Draw the eyes along the horizontal line and the eyebrows just above them. Eyes are essential for showing emotion.

NOW TRY ...
MOOD SWINGS

Faces are made up of different features – the combination is what makes up a person's facial expression. Try drawing the same face shape several times, then play around with different eyes, noses and mouths to create all sorts of expressions.

Happy

STEP 3

Add the nose and mouth
down the vertical line.

STEP 5

Add the ears, which should be
slightly lower than the eyes.

STEP 4

Adjust the shape of the chin and cheeks
to create sharper, striking features
or chubby cheeks.

Pay attention to different face shapes, which can really identify a person. Most faces are round, oval or slightly squared off.

STEP 6

Now pick a hairstyle to suit your
character. Draw a hairline to
guide where the hair flows from.

Sad

Scared

Cross

DRAWING PEOPLE

Now you can draw faces, it's time to try drawing the whole body! By breaking it down into simple shapes, the body is much easier to get right.

PROPORTIONS

Drawing people is all about proportions. You need to understand these before starting to think about how a person might be posed. Use these top tips to help you:

- Use block shapes or a stick man as guidelines to build up your person.

- Start with the person's body. You should add the head last.

- A person's body is usually equal in length to about eight of their heads.

Work in light pencil so you can rub out the guidelines.

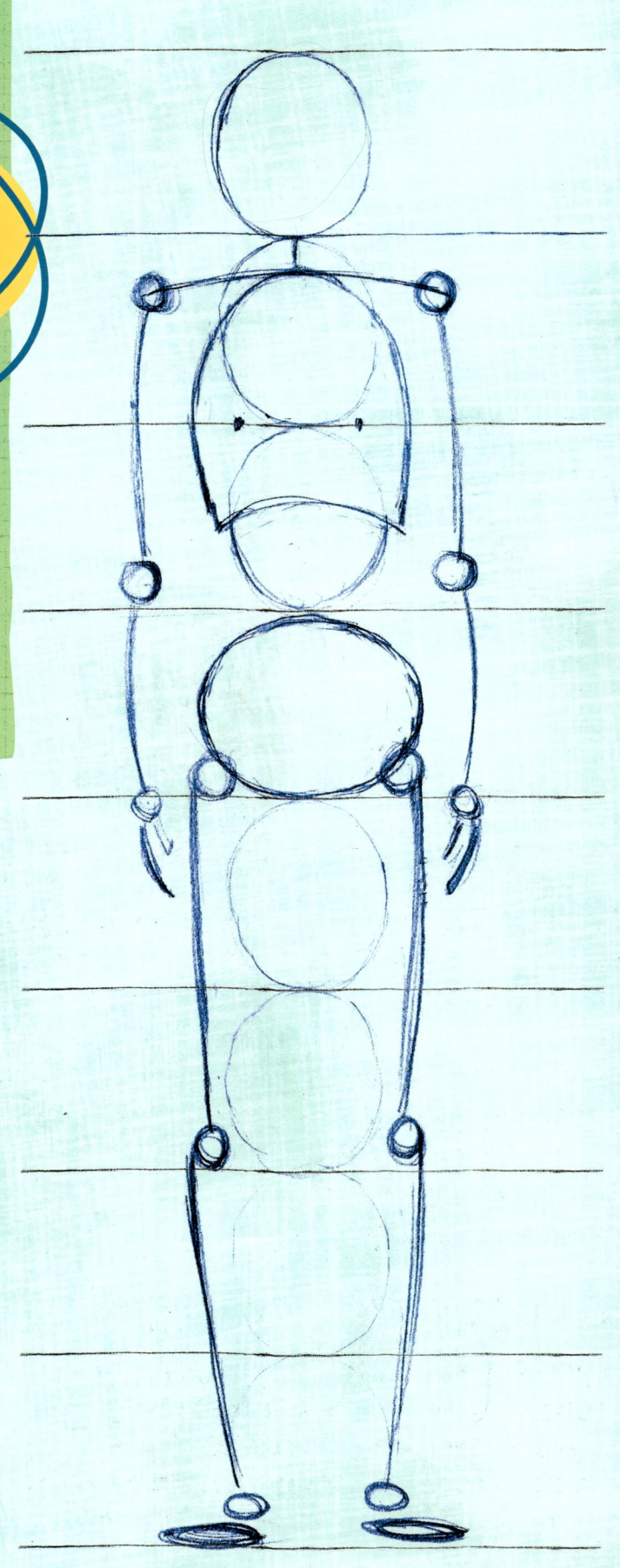

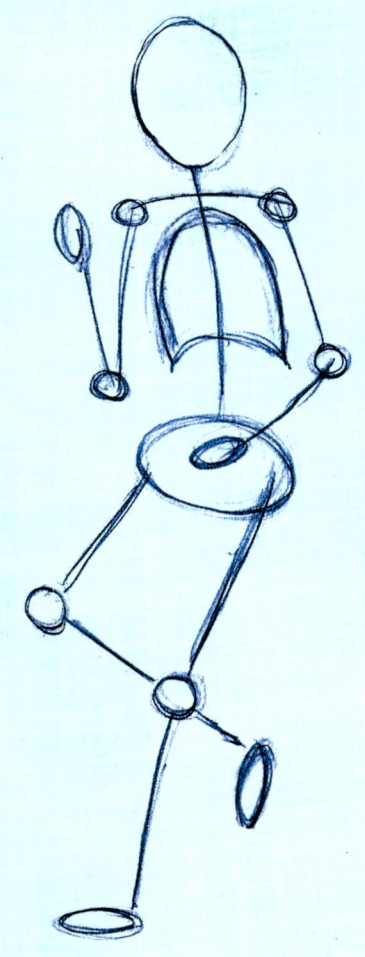

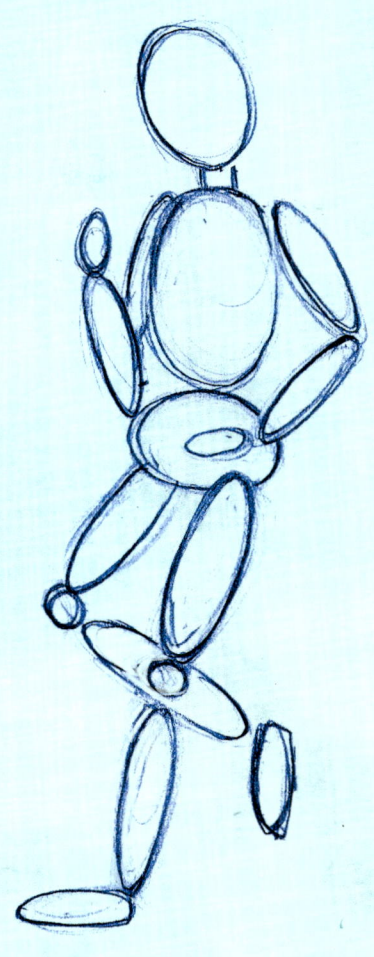

STEP 1

Start with two oblongs or ovals for the body, then a circle for the head. Add lines for the legs and arms, with small circles to indicate knees, elbows, hands and feet.

STEP 2

Now you can start adding some flesh and definition. Use ovals to build up the shapes of the limbs and fill out the body.

STEP 3

Use the tips on pages 12–13 to draw the face. Finish by adding clothes and some funky accessories.

NOW TRY ...
COPY FROM LIFE

To help you get used to different angles and body shapes, ask friends or family to pose for you. Remember to look for simple shapes at first. Build up the basic body shape, then make it come to life with detail and expression.

MOVEMENT

Movement and motion add action to your drawings and make them more dynamic.

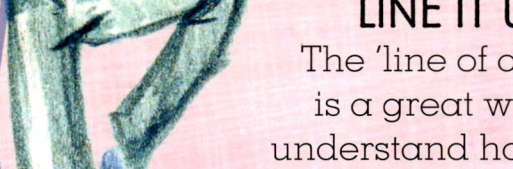

LINE IT UP

The 'line of action' is a great way to understand how your figure moves, and helps you to come up with good poses to give your drawings motion. Imagine a line running through your figure; this is the line of action. In a good pose, the line of action will curve and flow from one end of the figure to the other, clearly showing which direction the character is moving in.

Make sure the person's hair has movement too – pony tails, floppy cuts and fringes all move about!

GET ACTIVE

Try drawing your friends playing sport or dancing. Draw your line of action first, and then your figure over the top.

LARGER THAN LIFE

You can exaggerate the line of action
to give poses more movement and life.
Alter the thickness of the drawing lines
of your figure to add energy.

GO DIRECT

Add motion lines to
suggest the direction of
travel, or to represent
spinning, jumping,
twisting or running.

NOW TRY ...
MOVING OBJECTS

Try drawing a simple car. You can give the
impression of speed by stretching the car's
shape, which makes it lean forward. Add
some motion lines coming from behind to
quicken the pace even more!

PERSPECTIVE

Perspective gives the right impression of different objects' height, width, depth and position in relation to each other. Perspective causes things that are further away to appear smaller, creating a sense of depth.

Try recreating a street scene.

STEP 1

Draw a box with a line across the middle: this is the horizon. Draw a dot in the middle of the line: this is the vanishing point.

STEP 2

Draw an X from corner to corner through the vanishing point. These are called disappearing lines.

STEP 3

Now you can sketch in features using the disappearing lines to help plot them. Draw some trees on one side of the road and a row of buildings on the other side. Using pencils, gradually build up colours in layers to blend them together. Draw outlines and detail last, with heavier and finer lines.

NOW TRY ...
ROOM RAID

Draw your bedroom in perspective. Start with an empty room with a vanishing point. Fill it up with all your stuff, using the disappearing lines technique.

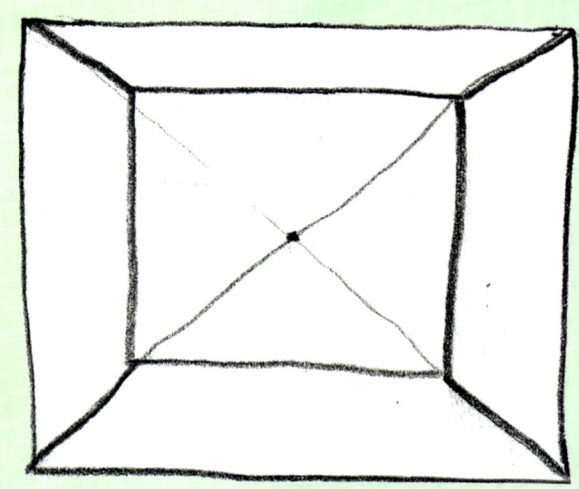

3-D AND SHADOWS

Now that our objects have depth, we can add extra lines and shading to give them a more realistic shape and make them look three-dimensional.

Let's start with a cube.

STEP 1
Draw two overlapping squares.

STEP 2
Now add diagonal lines to connect the corners, forming a cube.

Layer your shading evenly by moving your wrist while keeping the pencil still. Crosshatching is a great way to create shading. Build up little lines at different angles, and use thicker lines for the darkest shading.

STEP 3

Decide where the light is coming from. Add some lighter shading to the front and darker shading on the side.

CYLINDER

Connect two oval shapes with straight lines.

STEP 4

Finally, a shadow is cast on the ground on the opposite side of the light source.

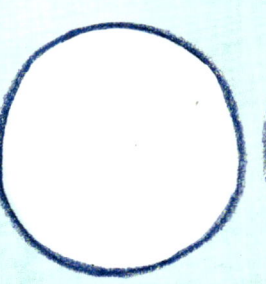

SPHERE

Start by drawing a circle. When you add clever shading, it is magically transformed into a sphere. Avoid using straight lines here, but follow the edge of your shape. Smudge your shading together to give the impression of a smooth surface.

NOW TRY ...
LIVELY LETTERS

Try creating some awesome 3-D letters that pop out of the page – these are perfect for signs and birthday cards. First, draw the outline of your letter, keeping it big and bold. Draw diagonal lines from each corner point. Following the shape of the letter, join up the lines to create the 3-D shape. Use shading to add more depth. Go crazy with your colours!

CITYSCAPES

Whether it's capturing the atmosphere of a bustling street market or the must-see landmark of a famous city, drawing the world around you is creative and inspiring.

FIND YOUR FOCUS

Choose a scene in your street or town centre, and try to document both the ordinary and the unusual. It might be the detail of a shop front, or some vehicles in busy traffic. Bigger cities have great skylines, with tower blocks, church steeples, skyscrapers and huge cranes!

BUILD THE BUILDINGS UP

Try to remember all the things you have learnt so far about perspective, movement and depth. Once the objects are in place, build up your colours gradually in layers of coloured pencil, which helps to blend them together. Do outlines and detail last, using both heavier and finer lines.

NOW TRY ...
DRAWING MEMORIES

Next time you go on a trip, draw the places you visit. Fill up your sketchbook with records of your adventures. This is great for your drawing skills because you can experiment with mark-making and new techniques. Even better, you will have a visual diary with lots of memories inside. You can stick tickets, leaflets and sweet wrappers in there too!

LANDSCAPES

'Landscape artwork' refers to artwork that focuses on natural scenery, such as mountains, forests, cliffs, trees, rivers and valleys.

Landscapes can be realistic or abstract and surreal. The possibilities are as endless as the imagination, and you can try out different pens, pencils and crayons for each scene.

Get started by copying a famous landscape artwork yourself: Vincent Van Gogh's *Wheatfield with Crows.*

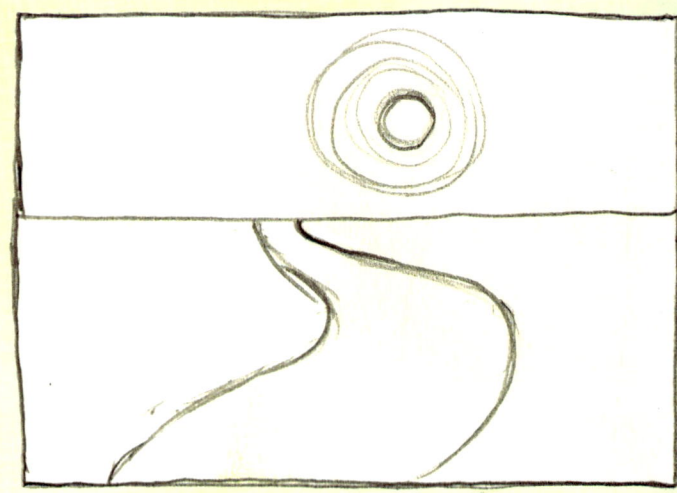

STEP 1
Sketch the basic layout in pencil.

STEP 2
Pick out mid-blue, brown and yellow pastels. Use the sides of the crayons to lightly block in the colour.

STEP 3

Add in detail with crayon tips. Draw sketchy lines for the wheat and road in orange and darker brown.

STEP 4

Add some darker blues to the sky and blend in white around the moon. Finish off by adding your birds in black. Squawk!

NOW TRY ...
GOING LOCAL

Try using some different tools for another landscape drawing. Blending colour pencils makes a wonderful seaside scene, or you can experiment with charcoals to draw a beautiful scene near your home.

DRAWING FROM LIFE

SETTING UP

Find five or six objects of different shapes and sizes: fruit, bottles and cans are good. Add your favourite toy or game to your collection. Having familiar objects will give you a personal connection to the drawing.

Still-life drawing is a great way to learn about observation. It is important to draw how objects actually look, rather than how you think they should look in your head.

Add interest to your drawing by putting some objects very close together and moving some in front of others.

STEP 1

Plan the 'composition' of your picture. This is the layout and arrangement of your objects.

STEP 3

Look at where the highlights and shadows are. Start by shading some of the really dark areas first.

STEP 2

Draw a rough sketch of basic shapes first. Look very hard at your objects. As you draw, make sure your eyes are constantly going from the object to the paper and back again.

STEP 4

Carry on building up different strengths of shadows. Use the side of your pencil for medium shades. Finally, add the details.

NOW TRY ...
OUT AND ABOUT

Keep a journal or notebook so you can draw wherever you are. You will always see something interesting to record or sketch.

STORYBOARDS

A storyboard looks like a comic strip. It's a great way to draw the story for a comic, movie idea or graphic novel.

STEP 3

Each box represents a scene in your story. Draw the settings and objects for each scene in a box.

STEP 4

Write a few words underneath each scene, then add speech bubbles near characters.

Use pencil so you can change things as you go along.

STEP 1

Draw boxes on a sheet of paper, leaving room underneath each one to add words.

STEP 2

Think of a story. Keep it simple, but make sure you have a beginning, middle and end.

Here I have written about a spaceship.

Take off!

Trouble with the engines!

Emergency detour to a nearby planet.

Will we make it?

The pilot's losing control.

Oops, crash landing!

NOW TRY ...
FLIP BOOK

In the corner of a notebook, draw a sequence of images that gradually change to tell a story. Start flicking through the pages: the images seem to move! The more gradually you change each image, the more realistic the movement will become.

NEXT STEPS

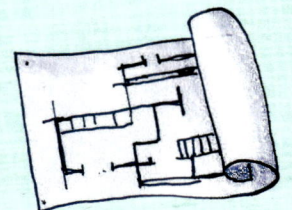

There are lots of different styles within art, such as Pop Art, Surrealism and Cubism. You can discover them by visiting art galleries.

There you can explore the stories behind famous paintings and the artists who created them. You'll probably find that some styles inspire you more than others. These will influence your own drawing style, so why not recreate your favourite famous masterpiece?

Drawing opens up so many possibilities to other creative things. With a great foundation in drawing, you could grow up to be an architect, painter, illustrator, fashion designer or sculptor. Your creative skills will be useful in all sorts of product design too – you could end up designing anything from a hairbrush to a smartphone!

GLOSSARY

ABSTRACT An art style in which the subject is unrecognisable.

ANALOGOUS COLOURS The colours that sit next to each other on the colour wheel.

COMPLEMENTARY COLOURS The colours that sit opposite each other on the colour wheel.

COMPOSITION The way a picture is arranged – its layout and objects.

CONTE CRAYONS Waxy, charcoal drawing pastels.

CROSSHATCHING A drawing technique that creates areas of shading by using closely spaced lines.

CUBISM An art style where the subject of the art looks fragmented.

DEPTH The relative distance between near and far objects.

GRAPHITE A grey metallic mineral used in pencils.

HORIZON The line at which the earth's surface and the sky appear to meet.

LINE OF ACTION An imaginary line extending through the action of a moving figure.

MARK-MAKING Experimenting with different tools and techniques to create a variety of effects.

NEGATIVE SPACE The background, or the area or space around an object.

PERSPECTIVE Drawing objects in relation to each other and giving them height and depth.

POP ART An art movement based on modern popular culture, such as TV, movies and comics.

POSITIVE SPACE The form and shape of the subjects in your picture.

PROPORTIONS The correct size relationship between different objects.

SURREALISM An art movement using dreamlike, bizarre combinations of images.

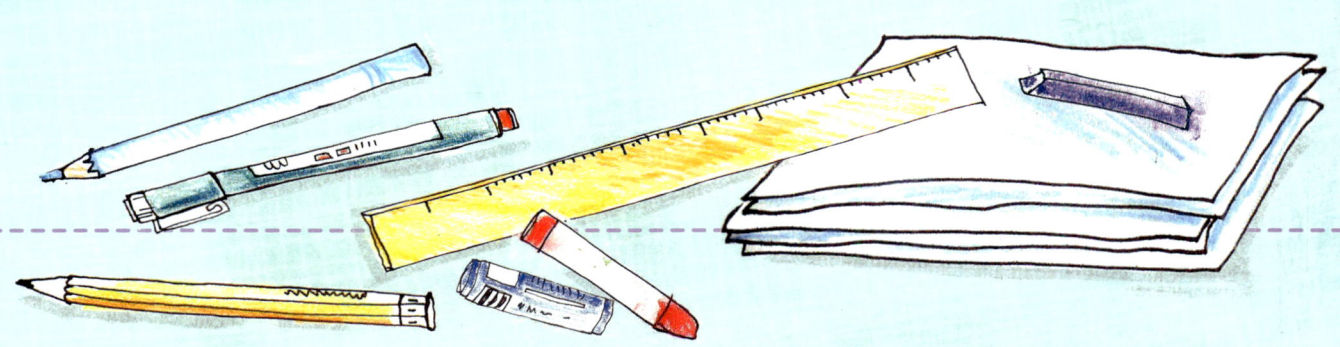

INDEX

First published in Great Britain in 2016 by Wayland

Copyright © Wayland, 2016

All rights reserved.

Editor: Liza Miller
Design: Simon Daley

ISBN: 978 0 7502 9841 4
10 9 8 7 6 5 4 3 2 1

Wayland
An imprint of
Hachette Children's Group
Part of Hodder & Stoughton
Carmelite House
50 Victoria Embankment
London EC4Y 0DZ

An Hachette UK Company

www.hachette.co.uk
www.hachettechildrens.co.uk

Printed in China

The website addresses (URLs) included in this book were valid at the time of going to press. However, it is possible that contents or addresses may have changed since the publication of this book. No responsibility for any such changes can be accepted by either the author or the Publisher.

MIX
Paper from responsible sources
FSC® C104740
FSC www.fsc.org